I Sing The Undersung

Elizabeth Bodien

I Sing The Undersung

Copyright © 2017 by Elizabeth Bodien

Published by Local Gems Press

www.localgemspoetrypress.com

For world musician George Glikerdas (1989-2015)
and mythic poet Blake Robert Poplin (1990-2016)

Eternity is the insomnia of Time. Did somebody say
that, or is it my idea?

--Charles Simic, *The Monster Loves His
Labyrinth: Notebooks*

Foreword

Dear Kind Reader:

Please consider, as you read on, that these poems were written in a marathon poetry-writing frenzy in a single month (National Poetry Month April 2016) with only one more month for revising and polishing. I am reminded of Lewis Carroll's words: "The hurrier I go, the behinder I get" as I ponder, and invite you to ponder, how our works might suffer and how our works might benefit from speedy creation.

Table of Contents

Prologue

This is a challenge you can try at home.
Find something not the subject of a poem,
like safety pins, or hubcaps, or spaghetti
or underwear (nope! done by Ferlinghetti).

The verse itself may not be laudatory
but if you look, you'll find an inventory
from poems about that famous kitchen sink
to verse about some creatures now extinct.

It's tough to find some thing as yet "unsung."
With "undersung," there is a better chance
for some things are significant enough,
deserving of at least another glance.

What Goes Unsaid

We don't speak out all that we think.
There's always more between the lines
and worth exists in words not spoken.
You need not speak all that you think
or try to fix what isn't broken.
To think ahead avoids landmines.
Best not to speak all that we think.
There's always more between the lines.

Stray Thoughts

What cock-eyed notions take up home in here,
this old and fusty brain that wanders wide
to parts unknown and brings back yesteryear
with such detritus, you would be horrified.
A junkyard, second-hand store or an attic
could never match the hogwash in my head.
A shrink would say the stuff is symptomatic
of one whom medics deem to be brain-dead.
If curious to know a detailed list,
you may read further. I'll provide one clue:
The numbers and the letters all insist
on changing places, just to rattle you.
There's more, of course. That bit is but a start.
The only thing to do is make it art.

A Humble Shift of Mind

When I cannot escape the ravages
of earth and my own vagaries of mind,
when I am caught between the wreckages,
we all have wrought, more mean, alas, than kind,
and see what good could be but what exists,
I take myself away to be alone
to where the old oak quietly persists
and music seems to hum within the bone.
This simple unassuming gesture keeps
a reassuring, balanced, even keel.
The problems are not solved, the earth still weeps
but something shifts, the lightness that I feel
allows the play of joy to bless the deed,
to make amends, at least to plant a seed.

Bark

I remember the smell
    my nose to its crevasses
I remember damp newspapers
    fibrous and crumbly.

I remember the feel
    raggedy sinews
I remember sandpaper
    coarse and hostile to touch.

I remember the brown
    the pale underneath
I remember dark walls
    the light moves within.

I remember the hum
    buzz of ancestor grubs
I remember the storm
    in its distant beginnings.

I Sing The Undersung

I remember the taste
    abandoned remains
I remember dead paper
    awaiting, awaiting.

Travelling the Grain

I want this vein
I take this vein
I trip on down
ooohh down and out
curving the knot

within the wood
to that far side
of its cool pond
I swim into
dark moods of night.

I jump others
to that vein
a path it is
I trust its leading.
I slink slower

breathe the beige.
do not tell me
this is no good
this is the heart
the soul of growing.

I Sing The Undersung

each slip of grain
invites me in
but where that crack
looms in my path
I skirt its edge

and with a prayer,
one wishful jump,
I clear the crack
land safe, ah safe
on that far side.

Humus

when animals
and plants decay
humus forms
it feeds the roots
so quietly, so quietly

beneath our feet
far from our thoughts
humus forms
organic, dark
such shapeless stuff

in earthy soil
or people's compost
humus forms
as fertile, complex
nutrients for life

green turns brown and rots
wet leaves stick to shoes
humus forms
one tracks the mess
from here to there

I Sing The Undersung

without agendas
as we know them
humus forms
and shares its name
with human beings

The Not Quite Lost Bond

The cow leaves the herd
asleep in the barn,
walks slowly as if
with no other purpose
to that low, curtained window.
She nudges it open
and with her wet nose
bends sweetly over
the deep sleeping child.

The round eye of the cow
sees the form of the child
under a quilt,
– the motherless child
with screams in her dreams.
Who called the cow
to this singular task
who offers the child
an otherwise dream?

Daydreaming

Compare yourself to that which moves in the sky—
the moon or planets, sun or distant star,
your whole self sparkling, not just a twinkling eye,
and as you think this, change who you now are,
no longer earthbound, you fly free and race
becoming primal in the cosmic swirl,
hearing, humming symphonies of space
and watch your hidden mysteries unfurl.
And if you deem this fancy or hot air,
remember all creation's made of dust,
the elemental pieces everywhere,
so go ahead indulge your wanderlust,
discover wondrous worlds that you're made of.
Breathe deep. Allow yourself to live in love.

Ermine, Ermine

Mustela erminea

The year that Christopher Columbus plied his ships across the sea, da Vinci painted *Lady with an Ermine*. What would that ermine say if it could speak? Can we know any creature's thoughts? Some claim to know their dear pets well.

The lady looks off somewhere to her left, the ermine's gaze looks that way too. They seem together and content but maybe for this moment only. The ermine's legs look muscle-poised for quick escape.

Shaggy Something Story

They could not recognize it
   hiding in grasses –
the furry pink creature
   with three feet, two tails.

Was it a freak
   anomaly of nature,
or extinct and come back,
   or an alien phantom?

They followed it,
   lost it, spied it again –
a strange humming noise
   seeking its planet.

They wanted to catch it,
   to see it up close.
"No, let it be," one of them said,
   "Would you like being caught?"

The thing climbed a tree,
   hid deep in the leaves,
humming, still humming
   while they tried to snap pictures.

"Unless we catch it,
   no one will believe us.
They'll take it as fable."
   "Well, no harm in that."

Yellow Ochre

Nobody knows why "ochros" should mean "yellow."
The word from Greek has entered speech worldwide.
An earthy pigment used as ancient paint,
at prehistoric caves, it's found inside.
On Lascaux's walls, a yellow horse remains
though ochre can be purple, brown or red.
Egyptian tombs show women painted gold,
no lipstick as today, ochre instead.
The ochre soil is widespread on the earth,
but not found in a child's first crayon box.
While other hues are chosen for the young.
the ochre's omission seems a paradox.

Hollywood Mind, or, The Must Pay One's Dues Belief

I will tell of all this,
these bleak motel days
when they interview me
on late night TV.
It will be my story –
the pathway to famous,
the hard road to stardom.
I will tell of all this.

Designers will call me
to offer their fashions,
magazines feature me,
bright glossy covers.
I will mention the hunger,
dark days of despair
in the article's details
that readers skim over.

The glamour is waiting
for me to pay dues,
to see if I'm willing

to endure these lean years
for my name on marquees,
my face in the photos,
my red carpet reward,
my big dreams come true.

Sequins

In secret, she digs back into her past
and finds the shoes that danced in better days.
Saved, they look as grand as she remembered
despite the dust, the years, the joyless haze.

The silver sequins sparkle still a little,
those tiny sequins meant for stepping out.
She dons the shoes. They fit like Cinderella's
and, for a moment, turn her life about.

Back then, she never recognized their magic.
They sparkled, yes, but she had sparkled more.
Now since he'd torn her life, their life, to shreds,
the sequins dazzle, rouse her smothered core.

A noise downstairs, her reverie is shattered.
The sequins are consigned back to the dark.
His drunken steps come angry up the stairs.
Again, his dreaded fists will leave their mark.

The Agnostic's Alternative

Somewhat godlike but not adored with ardor
(that one's too much to limit to a word),
this one's like Number Two so he tries harder
to do the miracles of which you've heard.
In fact this one can blow your mind with tricks
so you might think he is a superpower,
the one to pray to for whatever fix,
but one that you will disregard next hour.
So where's a soul to turn for explanation,
the one to thank for all our better days
and wonders of the world, of all creation,
that one we seem to need for prayer or praise?
If answers aren't forthcoming and we're stuck,
at least let's help each other through the muck.

Lapis Lazuli

burning the trash
in the rusty drum barrel
I'd rather think
of what is beautiful
– like lapis lazuli

the name itself
a delight for the mouth
and feast for the eyes
that sumptuous blue
replete with stars

imagine finding
in some Afghan cave
or high in the Andes
such a surprising blue
with midnight sparkle

fixed on the mask
of Tutankhamun
the same bold hue
selected by painters
– Van Gogh's Starry Night

I Sing The Undersung

the stone of royals
of writers, of seekers
celestial azure
with bright flecks of gold
the gemstone of truth

could we ever sing
enough of the beauty
the riches of earth
instead of our zeal
for all we will discard?

Natural Speed

Whenever she could, she shortened her words,
syllables cut, so "kitchen" was "kitch."
Her pace was intense, she walked at a slant
through each situation, for her that was "sitch."

As a child, I never could match her speed.
"C'mon," she would urge, and hurry ahead,
her speed the clip of her usual talk.
Were her ways taught, or were they inbred?

Before she left home, she'd whirlwind around
arranging, straightening all things in sight
creating some order in what she was leaving
in case she did not get back home at night.

Years later, I saw what can go unseen –
a natural speed that governs each one,
some slow, some fast, some downright frenetic,
each on a different rhythm to run.

Her Strange Enough Story

i.   About Herself

She would rather not tell it, a strange enough story,
but I can offer one or two facts. She was raised to
learn numbers but liked pictures more.
As a girl she rationed the words that she spoke,
afraid they might end before all of her did.
Imagining herself a fierce Wednesday hermit,
she dismissed all suggestions to live in a convent
sensing their schedule would be less than poetic.
A friend of the dead, she played the flute,
married, unmarried, gave birth to the future.
Descended from forests and ancient word wizards,
she bargained with spirits for the secrets of trees.

ii. Later

In an old musty shop, a forgotten back case,
a carved woman stood. No doubt her beginning
was human and loving, but time did its work.
Take her in hand and she may surprise you,
her outlook swirling from content to cunning.
Remind her of innocence of childhood or age
and she may compose for you sweet
haunting songs.

Daughter of No One

Let me be
in those silences
that humans keep forever.
    – Clare L. Martin from *Eating the Heart First*

It was always too hard.
Removing all mirrors
was a gesture of kindness
from Sister Elizabeth,
at the stone mountain convent.
With that she delayed the inevitable shame
when I tried later to live in the town.

There they rushed past me
flinging their coins
at my hungry cup
and without looking at me,
hideous me,
the coins missed the cup,
and clanged on the cobblestones.

It was always too hard.

I Sing The Undersung

No wonder my mother
screamed and abandoned me,
a babe on the doorstep
of the Angels of Mercy.
Should I be grateful
they opened the door?

And later, alone,
on the streets of the town,
how could I live,
ashamed of myself,
a horror to others,
useless and begging
for any old scrap?

It was always too hard.
And now climbing back
to the mountainside convent,
unable to stomach
one more day of abuse,
the younger nuns tell me
my dear protector
Elizabeth has died.

Abandoned and shunned,
abandoned again,

it is all just too hard.
I climb to the roof
of the towering convent.
Sister Elizabeth, yes I know what you taught me –
taking one's life, the gravest of sins.

Forgive me now… as I jump.

Unnecessary Advice

Zip bumba diddle wot
fragrant his pulse
zing da foof skiddle skot
love him, or else

Ugly he entered
zim yumma splosh
so what, said his momma
zill tilly dosh.

I love him plenty
jim jumba woo
riff dingle dungle raff
you love him too

The Undersung

Among us are the undersung
who care for others needing care.
Their own lives may be strained or wrung
while helping other lives somewhere.

More often women, sometimes men,
they cook and clean and wipe behind.
They're angels who make whole again,
large of patience, wondrous kind.

Jumble Sale, or, In Praise of Recycling

The lawn is full of things we do not need –
your skis you don't use ever since your fall,
the books I realize now I'll never read,
that childhood rendering of a Neanderthal.
We never plan to eat that turtle stew
that what's-her-name put up for us last year.
This bamboo chair now greening with mildew
will go without my shedding any tear.
As for that rainbow yarn some girl might want,
reduce the price so it will disappear
and keep some wearer warm in cold Vermont,
or somewhere else. Just get it out of here!
Let us become like nomads travelling light
till we amass new quantities of blight.

Sitting

To view, then to sit on, this barely curved bench
allows you to ponder the blessings of rest,
not sitting but assaying the mere act of sitting,
a pause in the frenzy of day after day,
to think before acting, to sit quiet and breathe,
maybe to dream, perhaps to remember
that one other bench where you both liked to sit
your small park in the evening
breeze-fragrant spring
brood shade of maples
burnt colors of autumn
bone chill of winter
to watch and belong to one season, the next.

Unnoticed, now notice your fleeing from grief,
to sink and allow yourself to swirl down,
into a vortex of ever, forever.
Your arms reach out but cannot reach him.
Your eyes see him vanish, vanish from view.
Your words fade in air, finding no home,
now that you sit and the swirl settles down.
Rest then, allow your breath its own seeping

into the void, the absence, the nothing.
Sense how it swallows you, makes you its own.
The mere act of sitting has carried you here
where you dwell no longer
in the love you deemed lost,
but begin, even swell, in a new bounty of love.

Untrusty Map, or On the Value of Sniff

Lost in a city, I gaze at a map.
　　Why can't I follow it? Streets are all marked.
And houses are named for the people inside.
　　Faint in the corner – 1762. Is that this year?

A raggedy dog peers out from an alley.
I hear him thinking: 'The years, they run
backwards and forwards, no warning.
You must find your way on your own by
your sniff.'

Sniffing, I find myself in a forest.
　　The trees offer clues. I follow their breezes.
Now just ahead, I sense a clearing
　　with a few people gathered, a scent of kindness.

A wave of contentment wells up from my bones.
　　I hum a tune as I make my way home.

Shoelaces

When
not
in
shoes,
they're
straight
like
flutes
or
coiled
for
sale
with
socks
and
boots.

They
come
in
pairs,
a
team
of
two –
the
way
I
wish
to
stay
with
you.

Hooray for Handwriting and the
Happenstance of Friendship

No magic really,
we simply started
at the same time
and same place.

Morning light flickered
and we rose together.
We learned our names –
their loops and their lines.

Trees kept our places
one day to the next,
our smiles constructed from
the same soup and bread.

Wanderlust,
circumstance,
finally duty
pulled us apart.

I Sing The Undersung

Now here again,
same time and same place,
unraveled, we knit back
some threads together,

our same handwritings,
the old colors at sunset,
glad for familiar as
we tiptoe the strange.

What the Dead Know That We Know As Well

You give us too much credit for our wisdom.
We thank you for your homage and your praise.
Your prayers, petitions, stir us very deeply
as we come floating through your nights and days.

We can reveal one truth which should be known,
the secret that should be much less camouflaged.
It's love, dear ones, that is the simple answer
to every question…if not sabotaged.

You need not ask us. You know this is true.
You need not die or seek us dead ones out.
But if you must, then take our words to heart
and live your lives with love, the guide throughout.

We hear you say, "Sounds easy but it's not.
What do we do with terrorists and such?
How can we love the ones who hate and kill,
who twist our love, those we can't stand to touch?"

They are the ones who need your love the most.
If you cannot get near, send love from far.
Seek common ground, a cliché true, but real.
Keep love in mind for all wherever you are.

Borrowing Words

i.

I can't remember the look
of my grandmother's hands
but oh her touch

ii.

blind ghosts find us
twirling their memories
scent of lilacs

iii.

in spring snow
I dig a hole
plant a box of secrets

iv.

such a blue night sky
stars tremble
old voices swirl

v.

she brushed my hair
with morning-sleepy hands
unfinished dreams

vi.
a soup
made with gumption
laced with dark cloves

vii.
my green velvet
wedding dress and shoes
twenty-five good years later

viii.
yearning
lays its hands on these letters
from the dead

ix.
in a nightmare
I step into a boat
sloshing in blood

x.
I am starving
for you to hold me
these long empty years

xi.

in the park
a statue of Justice
covered in bird droppings

xii.

warm summer night
instead of the hunt
owl sits and savors midnight's moist air

xiii.

I write in the dark
to the first dawn
that I will not see

xiv.

we would hear
if this window could talk
the dead people's chorus

xv.

my mother's eyes
the color of smolder
the same prayer intoned

xvi.
in winter
I dream of white oceans
blue sandy beaches

xvii.
at sunrise
smell of mist rising
the brooding pond

xviii.
a fireplace
of gathered twigs
gossip of women

xix.
no one can hear
night's quietest sounds
except night

xx.
the teakettle
whistles only one tune
cannot learn any more

xxi.
the shy girl
climbs the crabapple
composing love poems

xxii.
mirror, please show me
my eldest ancestor
I wish to thank her

xxiii.
dreading
this long, unplanned climb
I find mountain treasure

xxiv.
the wind rambles on
a forgetful grandfather
seeking what's lost

xxv.
what I knit
is what I build
stitch by impatient stitch

xxvi.
next spring
if I am still here
I will write this again

xxvii.
feet cannot see
where eyes say I can go
thank goodness they are willing

xxviii.

my third wish:

not to be greedy

and ask for more wishes

xxix.

the taste of forgetting

has no flavor at all

but a crunch most ferocious

xxx.

within my hands

a fine thank-you note

from the rest of my self

Praise for Rhyme Itself

These words designed to be in praise of rhyme
extol the pleasing sounds that finish lines,
and why, when hearing that felicitous chime,
we enjoy the order that such craft refines.
The art of poetry lifts us beyond
the common way we use language to speak
and offers too new prospects to respond
with music rather than the old critique.
Just how this works is one grand mystery
(while all acknowledge mystery's involved),
the best of poets throughout history
can write, and yet the question's still unsolved.
In spite of that, we still can honor rhyme,
the perpetual charmer, thespian of time.

Last Poem

This is for the not-quite silence
    after the mourning dove coos.
This is for the rhythm of air
    after Bach's violin stops.
This is for the faint smell of jasmine
    in the night of the clouded full moon.
This is for after your very last breath –
    unexpected and far too soon.

Notes

The connection of some of these poems to the theme of what is undersung may not be obvious so these notes are intended to clarify the connection. And "undersung" here means not only what might be valued more but also those things, like domestic abuse, which certainly should NOT be valued but addressed.

"Prologue" is the result of my discovering that there are very few things unwritten about.

Several poems address the value of pausing, and slowing down such as "A Humble Shift of Mind," "Daydreaming," and "Sitting."

"Stray Thoughts" sees some possible uses of the vagaries of the undisciplined mind, for example letting such odd bits and pieces be the inspiration for art.

Nature is certainly often written about but, in my view, not enough written about so there is "Bark," and "Travelling the Grain," "Humus," and again "A Humble Shift of Mind." Closely related is the subtheme of the animal-human connection in "The Not Quite Lost Bond," "Ermine, Ermine," (an ekphrastic poem) and "Untrusty Map, or On the Value of Sniff." "The Not Quite Lost Bond," another ekphrastic poem, was inspired by a still shot from a. 1924 silent film "Captain January," about a shipwrecked orphan taken in by an elderly lighthouse keeper which may be found at http://www.tft.ucla.edu/event/captain-january-1924/. I was made aware of this image by Sandra Barry of Nova Scotia who in turn knew of it from John Barnstead.

"Hollywood Mind, or, The Must Pay One's Dues Belief" examines the belief that one must pay one's dues in the form of difficulties and hardship before achieving success. I have not yet found another poem on that subject.

"Sequins" might seem to be singing the praises of those tiny little sparkly things but this poem about domestic abuse is meant to suggest that, as said above, domestic abuse certainly should NOT be valued but definitely deserves more attention and measures to eliminate it.

While there are plenty of poems, hymns, and other writings on deities of various religions, "The Agnostic's Alternative" takes a slightly different, less travelled road.

I have yet to find a poem that addresses the observation that individuals seem to function best when at their own speeds so "Natural Speed" is included.

"Her Strange Enough Story" is an imagining of a kind of magic that would allow shape-shifting between live people and artistic representations of them.

Both "Daughter of No One" and "Unnecessary Advice" encourage us not to shun those among us who do not match societal ideals of perfection, whether mental or physical.

"The Undersung" is also the title of a documentary film by Adam Larsen and the poet Heather McHugh which was produced in connection with Caregifted, an organization McHugh founded to provide temporary relief to those nonstop, long-term caregivers who could benefit from a respite. (www.caregifted.org.)

There is much talk and writing about the value of recycling but I have not yet come across a poem on the subject so "Jumble Sale, or, In Praise of Recycling."

As far as I can tell, the subject of "Shoelaces" is unsung so I offer this short, concrete poem about them (and about love). And "What the Dead Know That We Know As Well" is another iteration on love which may have more poems than any other subject but which, in my opinion, could always stand to have more.

The short snippets of "Borrowing Words" were written in response to this year's poetry month prompts from Quills Edge Press, some with more undersung subjects than others but the title – "Borrowing Words" – itself is recognition of the connectedness of human language and how each of us can inspire the next.

In an era in which unrhymed verse is *de rigeur* and rhymed verse often scoffed at, even forbidden in some corners of the literary world, "Praise for Rhyme Itself" attempts to give the currently undersung rhyme a boost.

Ω

I Sing The Undersung

Local Gems Poetry Press is a small Long Island based poetry press dedicated to spreading poetry through performance and the written word. Local Gems believes that poetry is the voice of the people, and as the sister organization of the Bards Initiative, believes that poetry can be used to make a difference.

Local Gems is the sister-organization of the Bards Initiative.

www.localgemspoetrypress.com